C000103792

TRUFFLES' DIARY

TRUFFLES' DIARY
A week in the Life of a Fat Tabby Cat

As told by Truffles
with a little help from
Sheila Collins

APEX PUBLISHING LTD

First published in 2005 by
Apex Publishing Ltd
PO Box 7086, Clacton on Sea, Essex, CO15 5WN, England

www.apexpublishing.co.uk

Copyright © 2005 by Sheila Collins
The author has asserted her moral rights

British Library Cataloguing-in-Publication Data
A catalogue record for this book
is available from the British Library

ISBN 1-904444-50-4

All rights reserved. This book is sold subject to the condition, that no part of this book is to be reproduced, in any shape or form. Or by way of trade, stored in a retrieval system or transmitted in any form or by any means, electronic, mechanical, photocopying, recording, be lent, re-sold, hired out or otherwise circulated in any form of binding or cover other than that in which it is published and without a similar condition, including this condition being imposed on the subsequent purchaser, without prior permission of the copyright holder.

Typeset in 12.5pt Lucida Sans

Production Manager: Chris Cowlin

Cover Design: Andrew Macey

Printed and bound in Great Britain

May I Introduce Myself...

Hello people, my name is Truffles and it seems pretty cool at the moment to write a diary - how popular are Bridget Jones and Adrian Mole? Before I start, though, just some background information so you will realise that I am, in fact, rather an important cat ...

I am now fifteen years and eleven months old, so I'm looking forward to a big celebration when, in a week from now, I reach the magic age of sixteen - roughly comparable to about eighty in human years. I'm pretty sure that my personal humans who look after me are planning something nice for the occasion. They do try their best and generally we get on well, but sometimes they can be so obtuse about things that to me seem simple to understand.

My humans' names are Sheila and Peter and I have lived with them since I was six weeks old when they collected me, together with my friend Tansy, from a refuge centre where we had been taken. I can't remember my kittenhood prior to that time and I feel it was probably quite traumatic so I have never tried to relive it.

Tansy and I were picked by Sheila and Peter, I've always assumed, because we stood out as the best looking of the bunch. I have an immaculate tabby coat in variegated stripes of co-ordinating shades of browns and tans and I can say that, even now that I admit to middle age starting to creep on, my coat is as thick and glossy as ever. Tansy, on the other hand, wore a rather ordinary catsuit in black and white longish fur, but in my opinion it was rather sparse. Still, she had a very cute little face and I suppose that's what attracted Sheila and Peter to her as well as me.

At first, and indeed for about fourteen years or so, we lived in a house with a very large garden, and even a woodland lake, in the heart of Cornwall. It was a paradise for cats. Apart from Tansy and yours truly we also had three other feline pals living with us - Lucky, a rather nice boy in a pale shade of ginger and white and Taro, a rather snooty aristocat, who claimed famous ancestors, and he did, I must admit, have rather unusually soft fur in trendy shades of cream and seal colour. Tansy and I often rather envied him his haute couture coat when the new season's feline fashions came out. Last but not least, there was dear Robbie, another ginger and white boy who, sadly, had only one eye.

We all got on moderately well, though Lucky was always my favourite and if he asked me nicely I did allow him to share my basket and keep my back warm. He always had rather a crush on me which was flattering, and I was not averse to the odd edible gifts, he would bring me. He may have had thoughts at one time of even daring to propose, but I soon steered him off that track as both Tansy and I had become celibate right from our time in the refuge. Still, it was nice to have his adoration and I used to notice that Robbie and even snooty Taro watched me with a certain amount of longing (you can tell you know) whereas they both treated Tansy as a naughty younger sister-kitten.

We had quite a houseful in those days as, apart from we five cats of all different shapes, sizes and colours, we also had to endure two other major irritations! One was a large St Bernard dog called Hennessy who was for ever loping around and shaking off his fur all over us and drooling over our heads when he felt affectionate. The other was the sound of a large, foul-mouthed blue and yellow Macaw called Geronimo who made our eardrums rattle with his screeching. To complete the menagerie, there were tropical fish in a glass tank indoors and outdoor fish in the pond. The indoor variety seemed unreal to we cats, but we did have a bit of fun stalking and frightening the ones in the pond.

Now, sadly, all my old pussy companions are all gone, and I even shed a tear when the slobbery old dog went to that big kennel in the sky, but I must admit I wasn't too sad when that wretched Macaw moved on to a place full of other Macaws and screeching parrots - how absolutely ghastly that place sounds!

So the humans and I have now moved to another

house in a different part of Cornwall. I must admit I do like it here and of course I am now the sole kingpin - or should I say queenpin - in the new house, and I make quite sure that my carers never neglect their duties as far as my welfare is concerned. I like to think they enjoy looking after my diet, coiffure and litter tray, and I expect - and get - lots of pampering too. I am satisfied that they know my rules by now.

I make sure I take good care of myself by getting plenty of sleep and only eating healthy, life prolonging food. I never exert myself more than is absolutely necessary (why keep servants and do things yourself?) and I do make sure I test their patience from time to time - you must keep humans up to the mark at all times!

Anyhow, now you know something of how I came to be here today so I hope you will find some pleasure in reading my diary for the week. It may even inspire you to keep one yourselves.

My Week -
Early Summer 2004

Sunday:

8.30am Was awakened from a rather nice dream - I was chasing a mother mouse and her three babies - by Peter stumbling down into the kitchen where I sleep. At least I do get a lie-in on Sundays as normally he rudely awakens me at the unearthly hour of 6.30am on weekdays - something about going out to earn money, whatever that is.

8.35am Found myself propelled towards the back door, my personal cat flap opened, and before I knew it I was through it and standing out on some dewy grass. He always does this to me - I tell you, would you like to take off your fur-lined knicks in wet grass early in the morning? Of course not!

8.36am I came back in.

8.37am Went on cat litter and performed. I like to see Peter's face when I do this. I particularly took the time to scuff up the litter so that quite a lot fell over the sides of the litter tray and onto the carpet. Then I sat and watched as he brushed it up into a dustpan and then made the top of the cat litter nice and clean and flat again. He was muttering a few words under his breath that I normally wouldn't like to hear in public, but when he glanced at me I gave him an encouraging nod and he got on with it and it was soon cleaned to my exacting standards once more. I don't know why he always 'kicks' against doing this particular little task - it is, after all, quite clearly detailed in his job description.

8.50am Now it was time for my weekly appointment with the furdresser. (This, again, is another 'hat' Peter wears.) He is quite good at styling my fur. Of course he's done it for years and he knows exactly how I like it. I've never been able to do my own fur - Tansy, if I recall, used to do hers quite stylishly, generally with a few carelessly placed knots in it, but Peter always then came along and undid all her handiwork. At this time of year I always shed a lot of excess fur and this, too, doesn't always go down well with the carers - they seem to take it as a personal affront if it settles on the sofa and Sheila sometimes utters those same words I heard Peter say earlier if she finds some of my fur on her skirt. I can't think why. I would have thought they would have been pleased to have gained some nice fur - after all, they don't seem to have any themselves. Well, my fur coiffing went quite well so I had no need to scratch Peter this week.

9.15am Decided to have some breakfast. I wish I

6

could choose my own food. Generally I like what they give me, but if I eat a meal up quite quickly they keep repeating that menu as they think I really love it. Not true - I like variety and trying new tastes. I now tend to eat a little at a time and make the plate last most of the day until refill time. However, no food is wasted in this household - there is an eager mouth ready to devour everything I leave (more of that later!) Today the breakfast was prawn terrine with a lobster sauce - quite lip-smacking really!

10.00am Moved over into the dining room where I have a rather nice rug laid out in front of the patio doors which gets every bit of sun going. A lovely spot to relax in. After a leisurely wash and brush up to get rid of the lobster smell from my whiskers, I settled down for my morning sleep ...

12.30pm Something awoke me. It was the carers going out. They quite often meet friends for lunch on a Sunday. Trouble is, they also quite often bring them back and disturb me. Oh well. I settled down again to make the most of the peace and quiet.

3.00pm Time to wake up and have a stroll around the garden. The cat flap was open so no problems there. As I climbed through it, the bell on my collar tinkled and I thought, "Oh dear, that'll bring my next-door neighbour round". He, too, worships the ground I walk on and can be a right pain at times.

I sometimes wish I didn't have the wretched bell on my collar and the rather naff name tag with Truffles engraved on it; they make such a racket clinking together. This all stems back to when I was young and had a bit of a reputation for chasing little things in the garden of the old house - so a collar and bell were clamped round my neck and have been there ever since! I think the humans thought that it would warn away my prey, but little did they know it didn't stop me that often! Now, I'm afraid I'm just a bird watcher, not a catcher. As I've mentioned the collar, I will tell you, reader, that it is a nice designer collar bought specially in Florida with the exact matching tabby design of my coat. Anyway, I digress ...

3.03pm As I thought, Pandy the cat from next door came limping along to see me. He is quite a smart looking cat who wears a smooth-furred black and white catsuit and I must say he does keep himself extremely clean and his claws nice and short. I suppose I ought to feel a bit sorry for him really - he turned up out of the blue to adopt his owners who live next door (though this happened when they were in their previous house) having been living rough following some kind of road accident that left him with a permanent limp on one of his back legs. The family took him in together with their other two cats, Bob and Ty - more of them later. They then moved next door to us at nearly the same time as we moved here ourselves - about eighteen months ago. However, several months ago now they acquired a real little hooligan of a dog, a Westie puppy called Oscar, and Oscar has really put Pandy's nose out of joint as he is so boisterous. Consequently, Pandy spends most of his time trying to move in with us. I am certainly NOT having that - no way! If I feel that Peter and Sheila are weakening, I quickly give Pandy several fierce growls and spits in their earshot to ensure that they are quite certain we would not mix together! I am used to getting their undivided attention and no way will I share that!

3.10pm I sat on the patio in the sun keeping one eye on Pandy who was trying to creep nearer to me each minute. I let him get to within four patio slabs, then let him have it - spits, growls and hisses - the full lot. I love doing that. It makes me feel powerful. He is really quite frightened of me when I am in this kind of mood. Sometimes, though, if I want to tantalise him, but feel a little more kindly towards him, I'll keep my mouth shut - but he still doesn't dare come past the four patio slab boundary. He's a bit of a wimp really, prat I think your human expression is, but there again we must make allowances for his disability. Not for him, I suppose, the thrill of the chase with a mouse or a bird, and, although he can somehow haul himself up and over our neighbouring walls, he can't manage to negotiate my cat flap. That, of course, is a bonus knowing that he can't catch me. On the odd occasion he has tried his luck and attempted to chase me or pounce on me out of devilment, but I have always just dashed in through the cat flap which has slammed with a satisfactory bang behind me, stopping him in his tracks. I must say that even now I can still put on a turn of speed when necessary. Comes from my careful eating and looking after myself, I expect.

4.30pm Pandy and I were still lounging around on the patio when I heard the humans, plus their friends, coming back. Pandy hobbled off somewhere and I nipped in via the kitchen to the upstairs study where I have my own chair from where I like to survey things and see who is visiting and what their credentials are before I decide whether to acknowledge them or not.

6.30pm Well, I must have nodded off - surprise, surprise!

6.45pm Had a nice stretch and a brief scratch and then walked downstairs to see who were the visitors that day. I hoped they wouldn't be staying too long in case it delayed my dinner time. Two humans I didn't recognise were sitting on the patio with mine, and they were all sipping Pimms (a most peculiar summer drink that humans seem to drink when it's hot; certainly not something I would like to pass my lips - give me nice fresh milk any time!) I kept an eye on them but avoided physical contact

- ugh, nothing worse than fat, sweaty fingers running through my neatly brushed fur! My people think I am shy when they have visitors because I usually hide away and watch from a distance, but I'm not shy. I just don't like physical contact from strangers. Maybe I'm too fussy - lots of cats I know just love being stroked by any old Tom, Dick or Harry - but I prefer to get my pats from family and very close friends only. You know where they've been.

7.30pm Oops - I was dozing again. The people were leaving and generally milling around. I tried to get into the front hall and out of the front door undetected (one of my aims in life, as yet unfulfilled) but as usual they'd shut the door from the main hall so there was no chance! However, in the kitchen I saw that my dinner plate was full so I settled down to a nice meal. It was salmon and trout supreme this time; not bad - I do rather have a preference for fish dishes.

7.45pm Well, that wasn't bad - it filled a gap! Time for a last inspection of the garden. As I went out of the cat flap I noticed Pandy curled up under a chair staring at me in that besotted way he has. I took no notice and once I had done what I had intended to do in my favourite place at the back of the flower bed, I came right back inside leaving him out there - best place for him really! Oh dear, that does sound rather churlish doesn't it? I must try to be kinder to him - he is not so fortunate as I am.

8.00-11.15pm Dozed on Sheila's knees while she and Peter stared unblinkingly at a box in the corner of the lounge. Well, I say "they" but he very soon seemed to relax into a more horizontal position and fell asleep whilst making revolting snoring sounds. How inconsiderate can you be? I never admit to snoring! Ladylike purring is what I do! I don't see why they enjoy this strange pastime of staring into a corner, but they spend hours each evening in this position. They are looking at a large rectangular silver-coloured box with peculiar pictures coming and going on the face of it accompanied by various odd noises. It baffles me! Occasionally I have noticed images of birds flying on it and this, I must say, makes it all seem even more odd, but this may be a pure figment of my imagination. Oh well, each to their own as they say - I will never understand the human mind and certainly they will never understand mine!

11.20pm Bedtime. Back to the kitchen again. My night bed was put out for me (in the daytime I have a rather trendy leopard-skin print bed) and I flopped onto it. The end of a pleasant day ...

Monday:

6.40am My usual wake-up call from Peter. Why he seems obsessed with getting up halfway through the night I'll never know. Perhaps he doesn't sleep well. He should try counting fleas - that is always guaranteed to send cats to sleep. Might I say, however, that I do not harbour any fleas on my person. The humans apply some kind of drops to my neck about once every six weeks and since they've been doing this rather strange practice I've never seen one of the nasty little creatures (fleas, I mean, not humans!) My vet recommended these miracle drops. He is a nice man and always admires me and says how well I look for my age. I say flattery will get you everywhere and so I let him give me my annual injections and worming pill with no problems. If my humans have ever attempted to give me a worming pill, well that's a different story. I make it as difficult as possible for them - letting them think I have it safely in my mouth and then spitting it out! I can play that game for ages and sometimes they have actually given up. So that's definitely been one-up to me. Touch wood, I have never had to have any treatment for illnesses so far - poor Tansy was always at the vet's surgery having to have pills and potions forced upon her.

6.45am I stretched and started to uncurl from my nice soft bed. Pity to have to leave it! Peter was busily valeting my toilet area and renewing the litter. Each time I use it I try to see how far I can send a pawful of litter granules flying - my record so far has been about two metres. Usually he misses some pieces and so I have the satisfaction of seeing Sheila, when she comes down later, also having to bend down and pick up the odd bit! Childish (kittenish) I suppose I am sometimes ...

7.00am It was a really bright, sunny morning so I didn't mind going out into the garden so early for a walkabout. The grass was quite dry and I didn't get nasty mud and grassy bits on my paws. Pandy was nowhere to be seen. However, a flash of long black and white fur from behind a rose bush told me that one of the other cats from next door, Bob, was on the scene. I am not too sure about Bob. He is young and in my opinion a typical hooligan who is too full of himself and is always trying his luck - needless to say, he gets short shrift from me. A hiss and a bunch of fives on his nose puts him in his place! I have caught him on several occasions peering at me whilst I have been performing private, personal functions on the back flower bed. A real little peeping Tom! Most off-putting really. He needs to find another young lady cat more his own age. I did hear the humans discussing him one day and they were saying that he is a bit of a devil -may-care type and likes winding up some of the other cats in the neighbourhood. For pure mischief he likes starting arguments amongst them in the hope that they will escalate into proper catfights. Actual fights rarely happen because after a lot of hissing and growling usually one of the cats will eventually lose interest and wander off. Sheila and Peter have a soft spot for Bob because he is the spitting image of Tansy. The first time I saw him walking along the top of our wall I must admit a shadow went over my heart too as I also, for a moment, thought it was Tansy resurrected!

7.20am   Time for breakfast. Not a particularly appetising one this morning - some cheap cat crunchies they had acquired as a bargain buy and some leftovers from last night - so I didn't touch it and retired back to bed for another doze.

7.22-8.45am Slept.

8.50am Sheila arrived in the kitchen and as I had heard her coming, I was up and ready to greet her. We have quite lengthy conversations, though neither of us is quite sure what the other is trying to say. She is utterly hopeless at understanding even the basic words of cat language, though she makes a good attempt of imitating the sounds I make. All that does, though, is merely repeat everything I am trying to tell her in the first place! I was saying that Peter's idea of breakfast today was not mine, but all she seemed to be asking was what was wrong with it, why hadn't I eaten it, etc. Well, I couldn't be bothered to try any more to make her understand that in no way was I going to eat it, so I just walked away. Frustrating really.

11.30am   I had been in the dining room in my sunny spot for a couple of hours or so when I saw Pandy come onto the patio. He ingratiates himself with the humans and is always asking for food, so I thought it was a pretty good bet that my unwanted breakfast would go his way. Sure enough I saw Sheila put the plate out and he polished off the contents in seconds. He gives them the wrong impression that he is poor and hard done by and they take it all in, silly humans. I know he is rather a sad character and I must try to be more tolerant of him and be nicer to him, but with regard to his winkling food out of people, I take my hat off to him as he has it down to a fine art! Peter is his main target. Pandy knows what time Peter leaves the house in the morning and also roughly what time he returns. He knows that he drives up in his motor machine and then opens the large flap at the front of the house in which the machine sleeps at night. Whilst Peter is opening this flap, Pandy limps as quickly as he can right into the space and hides under a second motor machine that also lives in there. He then refuses to budge until Peter fills a dish with food and waves it in front of him. In fact, what Pandy is given is my leftovers - as you know, it is bad manners to eat everything off your plate so I always leave a little something from every meal. Sheila collects these remnants up and puts them by for Pandy. He, of course, thinks the food is prepared especially for him, but oh no, it's only what I decide to leave for him. Call it my contribution to charity if you like - who am I to spoil his illusion? Anyway, Pandy's little scheme works like clockwork. Peter tempts him around the back of the house with the dish, and Pandy eats the food while Peter houses the motor machine. Everyone is happy. Sometimes Pandy chances his luck and manages to get two portions of food. If he eats quickly enough and can get back around before Peter has managed to drive the machine into its space, he then nips in again and the whole saga is repeated! Grudgingly I give Pandy top marks for this scam of his.

1.30pm Well, where does the time go? I must have dropped off again. It is so warm and pleasant in this room.

1.45pm   I strolled into the kitchen. Sheila was sitting at the table having her lunch. I knew that if I sat right by her and stared fixedly up at her she would give me some titbits from her meal, though initially she would tell me that she wouldn't give me anything. I knew better - the fixed stare always works and she relents in the end. Today it was a Scotch egg - delicious! Certainly a hundred times better than my bog-standard breakfast offering. I wonder why human meals always smell better than cat meals? And why, even if you have a full dish

17

yourself, the food on their plates always looks much better? I suppose it's a case of "the grass is always greener on the other side of the fence". That was a case in point, literally, a few years ago in our other house. I will remove myself to the patio now and when I am comfortable I'll tell you the story.

1.50pm   On the patio now. You remember I mentioned that one of my companions in those days was snooty Taro, the aristocat, pedigree Birman cat. Well, even he wasn't so above us all that he wouldn't stoop to some cat burglary! On two occasions he carried off quite spectacular coups. Once, we were all in the garden and as it was a hot, sunny day our next-door neighbour was also sitting in hers. Our humans were eating sandwiches but the neighbour had a nicely prepared pilchard salad accompanied by a bottle of that coloured liquid humans like to drink. All was beautifully set out on the table on a nice cloth with a napkin etc. She always liked to have things just so … Well, suddenly her little machine - through which somehow humans mysteriously speak to their friends - made a loud ringing noise so she went indoors to answer it. She was only gone for less than a minute or two. However, Taro, who had been on the lookout ever since he smelt the lovely odour of pilchards, immediately took his chance, leapt onto the table and deftly removed the pilchards, leaving the salad leaves intact. He was gone in a flash. A truly masterful move and one I have remembered with admiration to this day! When the neighbour returned to the table, for a moment she didn't realise that anything was different. Then something clicked - her pilchards had disappeared! Of course we never said anything, and when a day or so later she mentioned what had happened to Sheila and Peter they never had the bottle to tell her the truth either! The other occasion when Taro carried out a masterly theft involved a Scotch egg! Funny - humans must like these eggs as much as cats do, though what kind of bird lays such crispy-coated eggs I shudder to think. They must get very sore bottoms! However, I'll tell you that story later - I'm feeling tired again now.

5.45pm Goodness me - what happened to the past four hours or so? Part of my sleep programme of course! You humans should know that cats try to sleep for up to twenty-two hours out of twenty-four. That's why in cat years we live comparatively longer than you do - we conserve far more energy!

5.50pm I wondered if anything had been put into my dinner bowl (nobody had called me) so I decided to investigate in the kitchen. As I approached, a nauseous smell came wafting through the air and I could see some saucepans on the hob boiling away with clouds of white stuff going up into the air. I recognised the smell - curry I've heard them call it - so I knew the humans were going to be eating an Indian meal this evening. I can never understand why they want to eat foreign stuff. A good plain dish of meat or fish is quite sufficient and far more healthy in my opinion. I did once sample some Bombay duck. Now I am not averse to a nice bit of tasty duck and so I thought that I would enjoy tasting the Indian version. I nibbled it eagerly but, oh dear, oh dear, it was totally awful! Nothing at all like our own meaty British duck-tasting ducks - it was all dry and fishy! I spat it out - ugh!

6.15pm I had been sitting in my bed, my whiskers crinkling with the horrible smell of the curry, when suddenly a horrific high-pitched wailing sound made my fur stand on end and I jumped out of the bed, in my haste toppling over a three-tiered rack which stands beside it filled with strange orange, red and lemon round-shaped objects. I've often wondered what these peculiar objects are that the humans eat - they have a sickly sweet smell that I find very unappetising. Anyway, these objects decanted themselves all over the floor. Sheila was saying those words she shouldn't and then Peter appeared and started to get over excited, I thought, waving his arms about and shouting. However, he reached up to a point by the ceiling above the door and thank goodness the awful sound stopped. He very nearly fell over the debris on the floor - I rather wish he had, I like seeing how clumsy humans are. You would never see a cat trip over anything - we are much too sure-footed. However, Sheila calmed him down and soon the floor was clear, the saucepans were emptied onto their plates, the steam subsided and thankfully the smell did too. My bowl appeared with some nice chicken in it and we all began to eat. Peace reigned.

7.15-11.00pm Slept fitfully on Sheila's knees while they stared incessantly as usual at the silver box in the corner of the lounge. My nerves were still jangling from the upset in the kitchen earlier and that ghastly siren going off. (I think I heard Peter call it a smoke alarm, though he added an adjective beginning with 'b' in front of it!) The whole thing was really quite frightening for someone of my temperament and should not have happened. I expect to live in a quiet and well-ordered environment. Usually it is, but occasionally, like this evening, the humans trip up. Talking of tripping up reminds me of rather a funny incident that I had a hand in a few years ago. I think I mentioned earlier that from time to time we cats like to try the patience of humans - it keeps them up to scratch (pardon the pun!) When the gang of us - Lucky, Tansy, Taro, Robbie and myself - were all living together, one or other of us liked to hide when we were called in for the evening curfew. This would always infuriate the humans who would spend a needless half hour or more repeatedly walking around the garden calling the name of the missing cat. This game was more enjoyable when it was raining. Eventually the cat would be found sitting on the doorstep. Lucky was the past master at this game. We prided ourselves that not once did the humans ever realise that our hiding places were right nearby! They never spotted us. Really they were so unobservant; they had totally no idea - no self-respecting cat would ever lose sight of its prey. Anyway, Peter was shouting for me one evening and after about three-quarters of an hour I decided to make myself seen. He came rushing out and tried to grab me as I stood near, but not right by, the doorway. As he attempted to pick me up I neatly side-stepped, but he, carrying on moving through the momentum of his run, tripped over and fell right into the centre of a large, low flowering shrub growing by the edge of the house. Leaves and petals scattered everywhere - I also scattered! But I couldn't contain my laughter as he was totally stuck and had to be hauled up by Sheila who, I was glad to see, was also choking with suppressed laughter. To be on the safe side, I did keep out of his way for a few days and I was truly sorry that he hurt his knee, but I still chuckle about the incident even now. It was definitely another one-up to me!

11.10pm Retired to bed.

Tuesday:

6.35am Another unearthly wake-up call. I did not feel in the least like getting up this morning and refused to budge when Peter wanted to try his usual trick of bunging me out through the cat flap. I think he must have some kind of perverted sense of humour in seeing me tip-pawing through the wet morning grass. Anyway, it didn't work today.

7.45am As soon as I heard him leaving the house I got up and made my own way through the cat flap. By this time the bright sunlight had dried up the grass so it was no hardship walking over it. There was no point in using my litter tray as I wouldn't have the pleasure of watching him collect up the granules, so I performed my morning ablutions and toilet in my private spot at the back of the garden. Even that loutish Bob wasn't around to spy on me and I felt rather content with my lot and at peace with myself. I sat and just drank in the nice sunlight for ten minutes or so and then returned to have my breakfast before Sheila appeared on the scene.

10.30am I dozed in the sun. It being such a lovely day, Sheila was avoiding her duties and she spent most of the day sitting on the patio leafing through various celebrity magazines, though I knew when Peter returned home she would tell him how busy she had been doing housework all day! I told you that she and I have a good rapport so I would never give her away, but as you know, dear reader, cats are always very crafty so I could probably somehow contrive to spill the beans on her if she ever really upset me!

1.30pm Lunch in the garden. Very nice. Sheila had some ham sandwiches and I enjoyed some off cuts of the ham. I must say that she is a soft touch when it comes to giving titbits. Although my own food is generally very acceptable, as ever, humans' food seems so much tastier. I especially like that rather odd stuff they call cheese. Now, I have heard of a Cheshire cat, but I was unaware that there is also a Cheshire cheese - and very nice it is too!

2.15pm Whilst we were still lazing on the patio, Pandy arrived, though he took care not to position himself too close to me. In some ways I wish he did have a little more 'oomph' but I think he's never forgotten how I growled and spat at him when he first ventured into my space. I wouldn't really do anything nasty to him, but he must be kept in his place. I think I may have a 'Be nice to Pandy day' tomorrow. That will surprise him! I may even let him get to within just two patio slabs away from me. He will then be able to admire me from quite close - the lucky lad! I have noticed that recently he has taken a chance and entered our kitchen through the back door when Sheila's left it open.

(As I said before, if it's closed he can't make it through the cat flap because of his bad leg.) If I've been sitting inside the kitchen when he's got in, one fixed stare from me and he's backed out again. Once or twice, though, he's got in when I've been in the garden. He has at least had the nerve to explore a bit and once even found time apparently to have a kip as Sheila found incriminating black and white hairs on one of their beds! So I respect Pandy for proving that even he can be crafty when he wants to be- and, of course, the daily food scam with Peter proves that!

4.00pm I took a stroll round the garden. There is a nice little flower bed in the centre where the plants are embedded in slate chippings. In the sun these warm up nicely and are rather delightful to lie on. So, after the ritual of flexing my front claws on the log surround to this bed, I flopped onto it and made myself lovely and comfortable with the sun still pouring down. Throughout the garden there are lots of statues of we cats - a way the humans have of showing just how much they worship us. I must say it is a nice feeling to be adored and, credit where credit's due, I havn't had much to complain about with Peter and Sheila as they've looked after my every whim. They have tried hard to meet my exacting standards and, if I am honest, I couldn't have found a better human family, but don't tell them that as it will make them swollen headed! Dear me, I am getting very sentimental now, it must be the sun relaxing me! So ... time to have a nap once more.

6.15pm I headed back to the kitchen. With a bit of miaow talk I managed to get Sheila to understand that my supper was needed promptly. All that sun had made me feel rather peckish. In Sheila's case, all that sun had made her feel rather lethargic. Anyway, she eventually understood and a full dish was put on the mat; something I like very much today - mackerel in jelly. Peter and Sheila also had a fish meal - nothing like fish to keep you healthy I say - but Peter had to collect theirs from the fish and chip shop in the village. Sheila's lazy day was still continuing.

6.45-8.45pm No silver box this evening - they sat in the garden with me. All in all it was very pleasant. The birdsong sounded lovely, the evening sun still shone and all was quiet and peaceful. What more could a cat want?

11.10pm Well, another day over - a day full of nothing really but somehow I felt even more tired at the end of it than usual. I looked forward to a good night's rest and hoped it wouldn't be too hot. The one snag with wearing a fur catsuit is that you can't unzip it when you want to. Humans' outer coverings seem to come undone and can be removed if they get too hot - that is about the only advantage they have over we cats!

Wednesday:

6.40am Well, the weather was still lovely so I didn't mind getting up so early and I went through the cat flap before Peter even tried to persuade me - that must have surprised him! I am going to have a 'Be nice to Pandy day' today so I might as well be nice to Peter too.

7.00am Ablutions all done, I sat savouring the sunshine and the fresh smells in the garden. Pandy dropped down over the neighbouring wall and crept slowly towards me expecting my usual greeting hiss, but I kept my mouth shut and even managed a small version of a Cheshire cat grin. Pandy lay down not too far away and put on his adoring look. I preened myself and licked my paws whilst keeping an eye on him - yes, I suppose it is nice to have an admirer. I have had a few in my time - I've always been pretty choosy with whom I associate, though you don't always have to have a posh upbringing to be attractive. Lucky was the one, I suppose, that I liked the best - he was flamboyant in a ginger sort of way and always had a devil-may-care attitude. He was a farm kitten that my humans had rescued when he had been hit by one of those infernal motor machines. He was only about three months old at the time and was lucky (hence his name!) that they came along at the time as he was lying in the road concussed with a fractured lower jaw. Nasty. Anyway, after a visit to the vet's he was soon made fit and well and came into their home. At the time I was not on the scene, but when Tansy and I were adopted a couple of years later, Lucky was very good to us, showing us the ropes - like where the local vole and mice nests were situated (he was a great hunter, having had to fend for himself right from his rather inauspicious start in the farmyard) and where the best sunny spots were in the garden. He always had interesting tales to tell, including how he came to be adopted after his accident. But it was Pandy's day today, so I removed thoughts of Lucky from my mind and carried on smiling at Pandy, but he very soon sloped off somewhere.

8.00am   I came in for breakfast and then strolled into the dining room to spend the next few hours on my sunny mat. I could see Pandy outside on the patio. He came and looked through the glass at me. Usually I give a growl and flatten my ears when he does this, but today I merely smiled. This seemed to unnerve him even more than when I growl! He curled up a few feet away and we both prepared for our morning slumber period. Whilst I was in dozing mode I pondered over his rather odd name. Why 'Pandy'? I asked myself. Could it be short for Andy Pandy, some sort of puppet I'd heard Sheila talk about when they first knew Pandy's name. But Andy Pandy used to wear a blue and white suit; Pandy's is black and white. Well, sleep was coming - I couldn't be bothered to wonder about it any more ...

12.30pm   Well, doesn't time fly - snack time again. I didn't feel particularly hungry so I just picked at a few crunchies that were in my bowl. Sheila wasn't in today. Wednesday is her day for going into town, so I have the house to myself. She thinks I sleep all day on my mat. Silly human! Doesn't she know that humans' beds are just irresistible to a cat? I have long been accustomed to a Wednesday afternoon nap on their bed, but as I have always covered my tracks very carefully, they've never noticed. The tip is to resist having a scratch or a lick and brush up whilst on the bed as that leaves traces of fur.

1.00pm   Today I didn't have a sleep on the bed - the sun was so lovely that I went outside to join Pandy. By this time he was lying on the warm slate chippings on the flower bed, so I made myself comfortable on the opposite side of the flower bed. We remained in this companionable state until Sheila arrived home at about three. I think she was genuinely pleased that I had let Pandy spend the afternoon with me. I do think in a way that Pandy should get out more - I know that I have this fatal attraction for him but he is not very old and surely there must be more exciting things for him to do than lie around with me. Still, I mustn't forget that his leg prohibits him from any real chases, hunting etc.

4.30pm   Still sleepy, but I was in a reminiscing mood. When I was a bright young thing I was always out and about hunting or stalking, but nowadays I just prefer to snooze and remember. One incident that stands out in my mind is one that the humans often tell their friends about. It inevitably brings a laugh! The joke of the story is on me but I don't really mind - it even makes me smile still! It was a lovely sunny day, like today, when we were all living in the previous house. Sheila was sitting on the patio sunning herself - pity she goes such a nasty red colour. I bet she wishes her coat was in beautiful shades of brown and tan like mine! The big slobbery dog, Hennessy, was beside her, tongue lolling out, trying to keep in the shade, and Tansy was there as well, basking in the sun and sound asleep. I was under the conifer hedge nearby, resting after quite an agreeable morning when I had caught a reasonably large slow worm, and now there, just in front of me, was a tasty-looking fat mouse. Perhaps the mouse was feeling the heat too, because it was sitting dozing and foolishly not looking over its shoulder - when it would immediately have seen me! Dear me, the number of mice and voles I used to catch mostly because they weren't following the small mammals' safety code, which states that they should continually be on the alert for predators 24/7. Anyway, although I wasn't feeling particularly hungry, this target was too good to miss! I sprang into action. The mouse gave a startled squeak, but too late - I had already got it by the scruff of the neck. It's piercing squeak, however, had alerted the group on the patio. Sheila has always had a penchant for trying to rescue the creatures that we cats like to catch and she jumped up, saw me with the mouse, shouted, and started to chase me. Well, I like a good chase! We made quite a funny sight I should think, charging round the conifer hedge - me first, with the mouse still squeaking at the top of its voice, Sheila trying to catch me up, and Hennessy lumbering along behind. And Tansy slept through it all! After a couple of turns round the hedge, I arrived back at the patio and paused under the table, making sure that I had the mouse in a firm grip. Sheila and Hennessy ranged themselves opposite me. Then Sheila played a sneaky trick - she threw something to my right and, as I momentarily turned to see what it was, the mouse took its chance and escaped from my grasp. But then things happened so quickly that I was simply astounded and all I could do was gasp! The mouse made its bid for freedom, and leapt forward but in doing so it literally jumped straight at Hennessy - who had his enormous mouth open - and disappeared right down his throat! I remained frozen and gobsmacked! Sheila lunged at Hennessy and, putting her hands around his neck, tried to retrieve the mouse, but no, like Jonah and the whale, the mouse had well and truly gone! I really don't know who was the most surprised - me, Hennessy or Sheila! Tansy, amazingly, was still asleep. Anyway, I did hear that Sheila followed Hennessy around for the rest of the day but no trace of the mouse was ever found. Pity really, nobody was a winner and the mouse was certainly a loser!

7.30pm   Well, dinner was not particularly memorable but in this hot spell nobody was really hungry. The humans sat around in the garden after their own dinner and nobody said much. We were all savouring the hot spell and relaxing. Well, I relax most of the time anyway - as I said before, we cats never get stressed and wound up like humans seem to do. We have got the right idea about life - sleep, eat good food regularly, do as little as possible, and make sure you have your human carers willing and well trained. What more can a cat want?

11.00pm Bed.

Thursday:

6.30am   The dreaded morning wake-up call
from Peter. I do dislike being disturbed so early,
but because he seems to enjoy seeing the delights
of the dawning of each new day he assumes that I
do as well. He wasn't quite so cheerful this time,
though, as I had been up a couple of times in the
night with a queasy tummy - don't know why as I
didn't have much to eat yesterday with it being so
hot - and I hadn't quite been able to make it to the
litter tray! He was mumbling those unnecessary
words again as he shoved me through the cat flap.
No point going out now, I thought, as the deed had
already been done, but to keep him happy I
wandered around outside for about ten minutes
thinking this would give him time to clean up
around my toilet area. After yesterday, this
morning was pretty dull, chilly and dismal. The
grass was wet and horrid sticky drops of moisture
were falling off the leaves of plants as I brushed by.
This made my fur wet and spiky and did not put me
in the best of humour. Consequently, when I came
back indoors I went straight back to bed and,
ignoring Peter, curled up and went to sleep again.

8.45am   Woke up, stretched and went to inspect
the litter tray. Yes, he'd done the cleaning job
nicely, though a sickly sweet scent of flowers
prevailed all around the area. The humans have a

nearby cupboard full of bottles of liquids and cans of revolting-smelling sprays which they seem to think smell better than the natural catty odours I would prefer around my corner. Pity they don't get spray cans perfumed with fishy or poultry smells, which would be so much nicer.

9.00am Inspected my dish and found some rather tasty cheesy crunchies in it with bacon pieces. By this time I was feeling quite hungry, so I polished off breakfast in double-quick time. Feeling much more perky now I went outside to see if the sun was shining. Well, it was making an effort, darting in and out between the clouds which were scudding by at quite a rate. A fair breeze had got up so I found a sheltered spot by the wall and sat down to lick my whiskers and face clean after the bacon and cheese.

10.00am Pandy ambled by and sat down not too far away. But today was NOT a 'be nice to Pandy day' so I flattened my ears and growled warningly at him. He retreated to the other side of the garden table, nervously watching for my next move. Oh I must say I do rather like having this power over him! Anyway, we both sat quietly for quite a while, savouring the sun.

12.10pm A movement to my right caught my eye and it was Ty, another of the cats from next door. Ty and I have never really had much to do with each other. He occasionally passes through our garden to the one behind and we have only made the most cursory nods to each other. I know that Pandy doesn't get on too well with him or the other scallywag, Bob. I think that they are both a bit scornful of Pandy's disability and he, in turn, prefers to keep the peace and keep out of their way. Ty was carrying something in his mouth - a bird I think - but he soon disappeared through the hedge. I compared Ty to Lucky. Lucky was a champion hunter, as I think I mentioned previously, and was a really feisty character afraid of nothing and nobody. Ty seems to me to be of the same ilk. I have heard at times the sound of him and/or Bob squaring up to some of the other cats in this neighbourhood. Lucky had quite a few fights in his time and never chickened out whatever the size or tenacity of his opponents! One in particular, I remember was an extremely large, long-furred coal-black tom who moved into the area and immediately began terrorising the local cats, particularly the females. An abnormal amount of black kittens soon appeared in the neighbourhood and I used to hear our humans talking about this and the black cat whose human carers didn't appear to restrict him in any way. People nicknamed him Saddam. Lucky and Saddam had several skirmishes, one of which resulted in Lucky having to have a hasty visit to the vet and an operation to fix a scratch on his eye. One day, however, we heard one hell of a catfight going on outside. Sheila went out to find Lucky pinned against the garage wall by Saddam, both of them with paws striking out at each other. Trouble was that Saddam's front legs were a lot longer than Lucky's and Lucky's punches were all falling short. You human readers may equate the scene to imagining the boxers Frank Bruno versus Barry McGuigan in the same situation! Sheila's cries to break them up didn't work, but fortunately just then the postman turned up and, realising that the situation could have ended up pretty nastily for Lucky, he somehow managed to plunge in and grab Lucky away. Saddam ran off. Lucky, give him his due, was furious with the postman for extracting him from the fight which, of course, he insisted to me afterwards he would eventually have won. But even I thought that he was being over-optimistic on this occasion! Sheila gave the postman a cup of coffee, and I sat with Lucky and calmed him down. It was a long time before he forgot what he thought was the humiliation of being extracted from a fight, and after that he was for ever on the lookout for Saddam to get his revenge. However, if not to Lucky's, it was to the relief of the rest of us that a couple of months later Saddam disappeared from the scene. The humans thought that his owners had moved away. So that was the end of a chapter of terrorisation of the local felines by one evil cat.

1.30pm Lunchtime. My appetite was certainly much better today and I had a delightful mixture this time of cod and haddock with a piquant cheesy sauce that just tripped off the tongue! Pandy was also given a dish of this and he scoffed it in about ten seconds flat. Obviously unused to gourmet food, he should have savoured each mouthful as I did - makes it seem to last longer too!

1.45pm   After that meal I retired to the dining room window and prepared to spend the rest of the afternoon on the mat dozing in the sun.

6.00pm   The humans had an old friend who'd arrived to stay for a few days and, whilst Sheila was in the kitchen fussing over their dinner, Peter and Lois, the friend, were having a drink in the sitting area of the dining room. I was lying beside them feeling at peace with the world with Lois stroking my fur. She is one of the few people I allow to touch me but, having known her all my life, and knowing that Sheila and her have been friends since they were kittens themselves, I trust her completely. For some reason Peter and Lois were talking about ghosts. At this point I must tell you that although the humans find it totally impossible to understand cat language, I can understand a lot of their words. They only think I know simple words like 'dinner', my name 'Truffles', 'stop it', 'no' or 'come in,' etc., but they would be surprised if they knew quite what I did understand, and they'd also be very nervous if I could actually talk in human language because I could spill lots of beans as they say!

Because of the shape of a cat's mouth and throat and our type of larynx that isn't possible, so they can be relieved on that score! But I digress again ...

6.15pm   Whilst Peter and Lois were talking about ghosts, suddenly we all jumped as from the chimney came ominous rustling and whirring sounds. I sprang up and they both stopped talking in mid-sentence and listened - more whirring noises sounding very ghostly! All of a sudden down the chimney fell a blackbird. My goodness, manna from heaven I thought! It flew to the patio doors, but as I began to run towards it Peter did a leap forward worthy of one of the best rugby players and grabbed the confused bird. He opened the door and it flew out. Well, what a swizz I thought - that would have made a nice snack for me. Oh well it was not to be. The story of my life I suppose - missed opportunities!

9.30pm   Dinner for the humans finished and I was quite sated myself with the titbits Lois had passed to me under the table. They removed themselves to the lounge and started looking at the strange silver box again, only this time they seemed to be watching something from which I could swear I heard their own voices. Whatever it was they seemed to enjoy it and the conversation was all about their recent holiday. Their holidays are definitely not a thing I enjoy. I will tell you about that tomorrow probably - I'm feeling sleepy now.

12.10pm Finally to my proper bed. Activities went on in the kitchen for much longer than usual tonight, so I had no chance of any peace before the humans all, thankfully, disappeared to their own beds.

Friday:

6.30am Well, I slept much better than last night and never even had to disturb the litter tray, so I got a pat on the head and a big smile from Peter this morning. Smarmy devil being so patronising! Still, I must keep in his good books because it's my big day tomorrow and I hope he and Sheila will be giving me a nice treat! Silly aren't I, making a big thing of a birthday? Perhaps living with humans for so long is making me become humanised myself! Nooooh ... heaven forbid! That's the last thing I want to become. It's a cat's life for me! I went out into the garden and found it was another good day with plenty of sunshine already. Lovely. I examined the flower bed at the back of the garden, found a nice comfy spot and sat ... Bob ran past not even noticing me in his haste to get to the garden on the other side of us. The lady there puts out food for the birds each day on her lawn - nice bits and pieces of bread and pastry - and so Bob, who is rather greedy, always makes her garden his first port of call. I stretched after my efforts on the flower bed, filled in the hole I'd made - always neat and tidy, that's me - and strolled back to the kitchen.

6.45am Peter must have been in a good mood today as he spent more time than usual patting me and tickling me under the chin. Foolish, I know, but it really makes me feel good! I could sit and dream for hours with someone tickling me under the chin. Sheila quite often sits with me on her knee doing just that.

7.00am Ate breakfast and settled into the usual routine of whisker and face licking. In fact I had a good all-over wash whilst I was about it. We cats are very fastidious in our personal habits - even rather hippy, travelling cats out in the wilds will never neglect washing themselves. Another reason why we cats survive so well, as we don't let ourselves pick up diseases from being dirty. I moved on into the dining room to catch the warmth of the sun. Sheila and Lois joined me and ate their breakfast. I can't understand their need to use so many dishes for their meals. One bowl for food and one for water is surely quite sufficient. Another thing humans should learn from cats! Think of the washing-up time they'd save.

11.30am The humans have gone out for the day so once more I've been left to dream and reminisce in peace. This time, of course, they are only going out for the day. Sometimes they disappear for two or three weeks. Quite inconsiderate if you ask me. This is when they go on their holidays. As I mentioned yesterday, this is not a good time for cats. We do not expect our carers to leave their posts. They may well be going to enjoy themselves and get away from their normal day-to-day existence, but for them to do this means that we cats have to make a sacrifice. We are imprisoned in cat holiday camps. In my case I have to admit I go into a very nice, luxurious cattery quite near to where we used to live, but I will never let on to the humans that actually I don't really mind it too much. I let them think that I loathe it and I take quite a bit of pleasure in seeing that Peter, in particular, always gets terribly upset seeing me locked up. I draw on my full acting talents to ensure that he thinks I am suffering most dreadfully. Sometimes I've gone rather over the top and he's nearly cancelled the holiday at the last moment, but Sheila - being an astute female like me - knows that I am putting it on a bit so she's always persuaded him to grin and bear it. Him grin and bear it - I'm the one that's had to grin and bear it! When they take me there I am crammed into a horribly small wicker basket where I can barely turn round, sat on a blanket on top of newspaper, which I find extremely humiliating because it makes it look as if I am incontinent and can't last out for the three-quarters of an hour journey to the cattery. I really do not like going in this basket, which also takes me to the vet for my annual check-up. From the minute I am shut in the basket, therefore, I have always screamed at the top of my voice for the entire trip - non-stop. It does give me a bit of a sore throat but it also gives me a great satisfaction in knowing that I am annoying them intensely. Well, I do try to make them pay for the injustice of being locked in a basket. When we arrive at the cattery I am decanted into what is really quite a nice apartment facing a lawned square with trees and flowers. The apartment is on two levels. The ground floor has a nice-sized area for exercise, including a toilet corner and eating section. A handy tree trunk leads to the upper section where there is a proper house with windows and a door that I can get in and - this is the bit I really like - it has a heated floor! Really lovely to lie on, particularly in the winter months. At one end of the complex is a music machine and that is kept on all day long so we have something nice to listen to. I can see out of the apartment's upper floor to the fields and wood behind and can hear birdsong most of the time. So, as I said, as cat prisons go, this is a good one. The complex of apartments is always kept immaculate by a nice lady called Anne who I have got to know well over the years. I believe she looks forward to seeing me and she always takes time each day to pat me and have a chat whilst she is cleaning out. However, when I first arrive and go into the apartment, I still scream continually until Peter and Sheila leave. I like to think that on the way home they are feeling sorry for me and guilty that they have abandoned me. Of course, as soon as they are out of sight, Anne gives me some food and I settle myself down and make myself quite comfortable. It's really like being in a hotel - sit around all day, a bit of exercise if you feel like it climbing the tree trunk, and wait for the next meal to be served. Still, we are locked in and nobody has ever escaped from the complex to taste proper freedom. But, however nice they make it, there's just nothing like getting back home and feeling the freedom as you go out through your own cat flap!

1.15pm Woke up from a dreamless sleep, had a pleasant scratch and went into the kitchen. Beef on the menu for lunch today. Not bad.

1.30pm   Went out through the cat flap to find Pandy already stretched out on the patio. He didn't stir when I approached, though he was watching my every move. I couldn't be bothered to growl or hiss so I laid down a few patio slabs away. With a full tummy after all that beef, sleep was ever drawing near again. So we both slept a couple of hours or so away ... I did tell you, it's a cat's life!

4.00pm Had a toilet break at the bottom of the garden. Pandy also woke up and vanished over the wall next door. Maybe some of the birds' titbits were left on the lawn! He is always ready to eat whatever is offered. I know that Sheila gives him my leftovers each evening, though I hadn't left much today. Funny how some cats are obsessed by food. Personally, I have never over-eaten, perhaps that is why my figure is as good as when I was a youngster. Taro the aristocat could also never turn down the unexpected, unusual titbit. This may have stemmed back to when he was a kitten. When he arrived at Sheila and Peter's home from his posh breeder, so he once told me, his breeder had sent a list of foods he was to be given. These included pilchards in tomato sauce, chicken breasts, scrambled eggs, fresh liver and cream, amongst the more everyday sorts of stuff. I told you the other day about Taro stealing our neighbour's pilchards, well here's the tale of when he nicked a Scotch egg with somewhat disastrous results. One day Sheila and Peter had been at home lunchtime and Sheila had put their meals on trays ready to eat outside. She took Peter's out, but when she returned to collect her own, the Scotch egg she had on her plate had vanished! Taro had neatly swiped it off the tray as soon as she had left the room! However, it was to prove his downfall because after taking only one bite from it he decided to run off with it and finish it at his leisure. He started to go down the stairs but Hennessy the big slobbery dog saw him with the Scotch egg and lunged out at it, somehow toppling Taro back down the last three stairs. Crack!! Taro's back leg fractured! My goodness, then there was consternation in the camp. Taro gave a shrill cry, dropped the Scotch egg and Hennessy grabbed it and was off. He did, I think, feel pretty mortified that he had caused Taro to injure himself. He always was a very clumsy dog. He did apologise to Taro afterwards but I don't think Taro ever forgave him. Anyway, this entailed an urgent visit to the vet for Taro who returned with his leg enveloped in a huge plaster and bandage which made the leg considerably longer than his other three! Seeing him get around was as if he was walking on a tripod, and for the first day or two he kept falling over sideways. He soon mastered the trick of it, though, and was speeding around pretty well as normal. We could always tell when he was coming down the stairs as we heard the bumpety-bump of the plastered leg coming down behind him! I am pleased to say that three weeks later the plaster was removed and his leg was as good as new. Taro kept out of Hennessy's way after that incident and I don't recall him ever stealing any more Scotch eggs!

6.30pm All the humans had returned from their day out. Sheila and Lois had been visiting together with thousands of other humans in some kind of enormous garden under plastic domes - 'The Eden Project' they called it, but the only Eden I ever recall hearing about had only two people in it and a snake and an apple. Peter had returned from earning money - don't know why humans lay such store on getting money; cats get on very well without it.

9.00pm Well, all of us, human and feline, were sat down feeling full after our dinners. Pandy was with us outside in the garden and it was still pleasantly warm, the sun only just starting to dim a little. The humans chatted and we cats dozed. What's new?

11.30pm   Bedtime again. How time rolls by - it hardly seems a day goes by before it's time to sleep again ...

Saturday:

8.30am   Well, I was wide awake when Peter came down into the kitchen - after all, this was my big day! I was rewarded with an extra-long pat and caress from him and I then went outside and was pleased to see that the sun had put his hat on especially for me and all was bright and lovely in the garden. The sun shines on the blessed so they say, and in my case that's very true! I do feel blessed with a comfortable home and caring humans. Many cats struggle to survive in horrible circumstances or have to fend for themselves in a wide world populated with many very frightening things and uncaring humans, but, as I said, I am one of the lucky ones. I found a super family. But I mustn't get maudlin just because I've reached the milestone age of sixteen. I am only going to admit to just arriving towards old age - I feel I'm only in the departure lounge now, not out on the runway yet! There are many more years in me to come! As I was carrying out my ablutions on the flower bed Bob and Ty strolled by, so for once I nodded and smiled at them and they, in turn, gave a couple of cheery miaows in return.

8.35am   Back in the kitchen and Peter had brush in hand ready to style my fur for my special day. I had to look my best! Sheila then appeared and made a great fuss of me, kissing me (ugh!), and she excitedly produced an enormous birthday card for me (humans seem to have this habit of giving each other these cards, though it seems a bit silly to me as you can't eat a birthday card). Anyway it appeared to be a large picture of a tabby cat not unlike myself and they had obviously taken much trouble over choosing this card, so I pretended I was very pleased with it and purred loudly as they stood it near my breakfast bowl. However, I was more concerned that at the moment the bowl stood empty. I was not to be disappointed though as Sheila busied herself filling it up with crabmeat! Wow, my absolute favourite! I felt this was going to be a day to remember - it was certainly starting off well!

9.30am   The humans and their friend Lois were seated at the dining room table having their breakfast and I was basking in the sun in my favourite spot. From their conversation it appeared that some more friends of theirs were due to arrive shortly, so it seemed that we would have a houseful to celebrate my birthday! Looking through the glass of the patio doors, I suddenly saw Pandy. He was clutching what looked like a bird in his mouth and indicating that I should come outside. I got up and ran out into the kitchen and through the cat flap. Pandy laid the bird at my feet. How very sweet of him to give me such a nice present on my birthday. A tear almost came into my eye, but I blinked it away. I mustn't let him know that underneath my sometimes prickly exterior I do have a big soft spot for him. I was amazed that he had even got hold of a bird as I would have thought he was unable to move quickly enough to catch anything. Whilst we were sitting there with the bird, the humans came out and that spoilsport, Peter, took the bird away exclaiming that Pandy certainly had not caught it; he must have just picked it up from somewhere perhaps because it was injured or somebody else had already killed it. A bit of a slur on Pandy's capabilities, I suppose, though very likely true. But in the event it was a lovely thought of Pandy to get hold of the bird - however he managed to do it - and I felt very touched by it.

10.30am Everyone was now sitting on the sunny patio and Sheila and Peter presented me with their present. Well, blow me, it was a lovely heated pad for my bed! They know how much I like the heated bed pads at the holiday camp - sometimes when it's been time to go home they've had to drag me off the pad! Although at this time of the year it wouldn't be used, in the winter months it would be lovely and I knew I would spend many happy, sleepy hours on it. Lois then produced a big pack of mixed tins of the very best make of cat food from some superior store in Knightsbridge in London (so it said on the labels). She gave both Pandy and I a taster and it was certainly whisker-licking delicious I can tell you! We both begged for more but to no avail I'm afraid.

11.45am   I had gone indoors and was sitting on my favourite chair in Sheila's study when suddenly there was the cacophonous sound of the front doorbell - there must be more chimes than Big Ben in that bell! All the humans were milling around in the downstairs hall, greeting their visitors. The man was flailing his arms about and talking in a most odd accent that I'd never heard before, certainly nothing like the Cornish accents I am used to hearing. I did hear Sheila tell Lois that the newcomers were from somewhere called Essex. The woman was also speaking in the same strange tones. Usually I keep my distance when newcomers arrive, but as this was a special day I decided to go down and investigate. My goodness, the woman was very tall - seemed like a giant to a cat-sized person like me - and she had extremely large feet which at one point nearly crushed me. I decided, though, that they seemed nice, friendly people so as an honour I allowed them to pat me.

12.15pm   By this time everyone had moved out into the garden again and the humans were sitting on the patio chairs drinking evil-smelling coloured liquids from a variety of bottles and cans and eating sandwiches and a local favourite, Cornish pasties. Pandy and I were sitting in the sun near to Lois, who was sneaking little bits of pasty to us from time to time. She's good like that. The visitors were all talking rapidly and the words 'ham' and 'eels' caught my attention. Now I am very partial to a nice bit of ham. However, the man kept on talking about how the ham had played recently and I thought, well you eat ham, you don't play with it, what is he talking about! He also kept referring to west ham. I couldn't imagine what he meant - west ham? Does that mean there is an east ham, a south ham and a north ham? It baffled me. Pandy, who doesn't know nearly as much human vocabulary as I do, hadn't a clue what they were on about! Then they started saying how much they liked to eat their own local delicacy - jellied eels. Well, I certainly know about eels, but there again, jellied? What did they mean? As far as I know humans eat jelly which is sweet and fruity-tasting stuff, coloured green or red or yellow. Once, I tried a bit that someone had spilt but it was not at all to my taste. I can't think how a large wriggling eel would let itself be put into a jelly! We used to get eels in the pond at our previous house. I believe they can cross land for short distances and had probably come from the stream that ran through the field next to our garden. Lucky and I quite often used to catch an eel - though they were such slippery devils that it was rarely that we could hold onto one long enough to be able to eat it. We also had some other rather strange land creatures similar to eels in that garden called slow worms. They were great fun to play with because they were easy to catch and you could bite off the end bit and then the two bits would wriggle separately! They used to keep we cats amused for hours. I would often smuggle one (in pieces) indoors to give Sheila a fright. It was worth the telling-off I got seeing her jump up and screech when she trod on one of the wriggly pieces I'd carefully placed on the floor!

3.00pm Peace again - the humans had all gone out. Pandy and I remained sleeping in the garden. I was feeling so content that I almost enjoyed him being alongside me!

6.30pm The house was full of humans again - they seemed to be everywhere. And so noisy all together with music playing and the clinking of glasses again. It seemed to me that the more they drank of the sickly-smelling stuff in those glasses, the more they all seemed to be laughing. Really it was enough to give you a headache. Anyway, Sheila called me into the kitchen and there was the Essex lady all excited with a jar in her hands. She tipped the contents into my dinner bowl saying that it was my birthday treat from them - jellied eels. I looked in the bowl. At least there was no red or green jelly in it. I sniffed at it suspiciously. It didn't smell that bad, but not that good either. As they were anxiously looking at me for some reaction, I decided to take a bite. Well it was certainly an acquired taste, but not as bad as I'd imagined. I'd eaten bits of raw eel, of course, straight from the pond, but not eel preserved in this special way. I ate about half of it which seemed to make the Essex lady very happy. Well, it was kind of her to bring it specially for me but, to be honest, give me a Cornish crab any day! Still, I expect humans in Essex eat very differently from those in Cornwall.

9.30pm The humans had just about finished their dinner and the table was littered with plates, bowls and glasses. I say again, why on earth do they use so many bowls? One each would be sufficient. Cats do not have to spend hours washing up or clearing tables; that's how sensible we are - one bowl per cat. If Sheila thought the same way, she'd only have had to wash up five bowls and five glasses - a two-minute job - rather than having a full dishwasher after just one meal!

11.55pm Well, at last the humans all departed upstairs to bed down for the night and it was peace for me. Listening to them talking and laughing non-stop for the last few hours was keeping me from sleeping and beginning to make my eardrums rattle! But they had all patted me and wished me a happy birthday and the nice thing was, I knew they meant it. I laid down on my bed thinking what a good day it had been and how lucky I had been with my birthday treats. All in all it has been a very good week and I will remember this special day in particular.

Well, I do hope you have enjoyed reading my diary - I look forward to tomorrow and all the other days ahead. I may even become closer to Pandy, you never know.